At home

À la maison

ah lah may*zoh*

Illustrated by Clare Beaton

Illustré par Clare Beaton

b small publishing

door

la porte

lah port

window

la fenêtre

lah fe*net*r'

chair

la chaise

lah shez

table

la table

lah tahbl'

bed

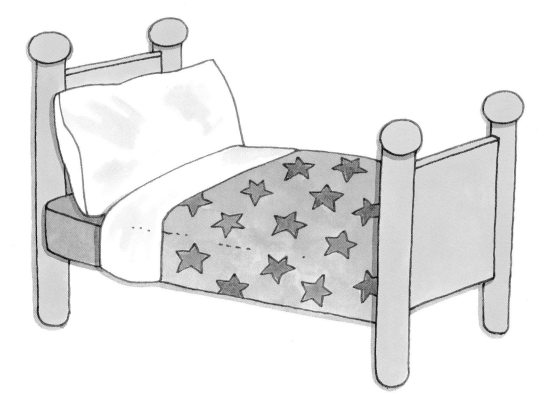

le lit

ler lee

bath

le bain

ler bah

fridge

le frigo

ler free*goh*

television

la télévision

lah teh-leh-veezee*oh*

telephone

le téléphone

ler teh-leh-*fon*

cupboard

l'armoire

larm*wah*

clock

la pendule

lah pond-*yule*

A simple guide to pronouncing the French words

- Read this guide as naturally as possible, as if it were standard British English.
- Put stress on the letters in *italics* e.g. lah pond-*yule*
- Don't roll the r at the end of the word, e.g. in the French word le (the): ler.

la porte	lah port	**door**
la fenêtre	lah fe*netr*'	**window**
la chaise	lah shez	**chair**
la table	lah tahbl'	**table**
le lit	ler lee	**bed**
le bain	ler bah	**bath**
le frigo	ler free*goh*	**fridge**
la télévision	lah teh-leh-veezee*oh*	**television**
le téléphone	ler teh-leh-*fon*	**telephone**
l'armoire	larm*wah*	**cupboard**
la pendule	lah pond-*yule*	**clock**

Published by b small publishing, Pinewood, 3a Coombe Ridings, Kingston-upon-Thames, Surrey KT2 7JT.
© b small publishing, 2001
1 2 3 4 5
Design: *Lone Morton*   Editorial: *Catherine Bruzzone* and *Olivia Norton*   Production: *Grahame Griffiths* and *Olivia Norton*
Colour reproduction: Reed Digital, Ipswich. Printed in Hong Kong by Wing King Tong Co. Ltd.
ISBN 1 874735 88 3
British Library Cataloguing-in-Publication Data.
A catalogue record for this book is available from the British Library.